# Tarot & Nakshatras

Sourabh Roy

# Copyright

Copyright © 2021 Sourabh Roy

**What you see is all there is -**

Daniel Kahneman (Thinking, fast and slow)

# Contents

Dedicated to all the blacksmith.

# Foreword

**O**nce there was a blacksmith and a serpent. The serpent had intuitive gifts (psychic) which it used at its whims and fancies. It invaded peoples' sacred temple(mind) with least bothered about dharma; when to use such gift and when not to. There was much furore among the common folks because of the serpent's growing ambition. Nonetheless, the folks agreed to part with something to the serpent for their peace. Mostly, the barter involved giving gold to the serpent. As nature's mysterious ways of intertwining paths, one day the serpent met the blacksmith. The blacksmith didn't have any gold but had something way more precious the serpent could ever imagine. The serpent as usual tried to invade his mind, to its surprise the blacksmith had few moves up his sleeve. A chain made of iron to trap the serpent in its own game. When the serpent couldn't move, the blacksmith used his sword to cut its head. This book offers a path to all such blacksmith who are not intuitively gifted(psychic) but can still be intuitive. All they have to know is how to see!

## Beginner's guide: How to read this book

A reader must be aware of Tarot cards specifically Rider-Waite Tarot deck and a fair understanding of astrological houses as well as nakshatras.

This book gives a different perspective on the archetype of Rider-Waite Tarot deck. It shows the uncanny resemblance of nakshatras working day in day out with all of our lives as well as tries to bridge the gap among faiths, after all we are not so different, maybe a little!

There are twelve zodiac signs namely:

**Aries, Taurus, Gemini, Cancer, Leo, Virgo, Libra, Scorpio, Sagittarius, Capricorn, Aquarius, Pisces.**

And there are twelve houses in astrology each with a significance:

**1st house:** self, ascendant, appearance, vigour, innate nature etc.

**2nd house:** speech (vocal cords), wealth, values, food etc.

**3rd house:** brothers, sisters, communication, short journey, neighbour etc.

**4th house:** mother, relatives, land and houses, happiness etc.

**5th house:** knowledge, primary learning, children, creativity, royalty etc.

**6th house:** debts, known enemies, maternal uncle, obstacles etc.

**7th house:** spouse/partner, trading partnership, death /transformation etc.

**8th house:** longevity, hidden enemies, occult, inheritance etc.

**9th house:** fortunes, religion, higher learning, long distance travel, father/father figure etc.

**10th house:** profession(livelihood), royalty, fame etc.

**11th house:** income, gains, pets, prosperity etc.

**12th house:** expenses, emancipation, isolation etc.

Nakshatra are the lunar mansions used in Vedic astrology. It is the elliptical path ('Naks' -sky, 'Shetra' - area/map) of the moon through the stars. Moon cycle is of 27.3 days; the time it takes to travel through its orbit. Considering equal divisions of 27 lunar mansions of the $360^0$ zodiac, each nakshatra spans out over $13.33^0$ which are further divided into four padas (legs signified as Dharma, Artha, Kama and Moksha).

The **27 Nakshtaras** (lunar constellation) are; **Ashwini, Bharani, Krittika, Rohini, Mrigasira, Ardra, Punarvasu, Pushya, Ashlesha,**

**Magha, Purva Phalguni, Uttara Phalguni, Hasta, Chitra, Swati, Vishakha, Anuradha, Jyestha, Mula, Purva Asadha, Uttara Asadha, Shravana, Dhanistha, Satabhishaj, Purva Bhadrapada, Uttara Bhadrapada, Revati.**

The 27 nakshatras and their themes are associated with Hindu mythological stories which repeat itself overtime. If an event repeat itself once or twice it's a coincidence (or an outlier) but when it happens over and over again then it becomes eternal. Themes of nakshtaras are not only applicable to mortals but even to Devas (Angels) and Asuras (Demons). To delve into the themes of nakshatra, it would require a series of book of its own which is beyond the scope of this book. Inquisitive readers are advised to do their own research on Nakshatras.

A brief note on Rider-Waite Tarot deck: It was created by Arthur Edward Waite and Pamela Colman Smith. In this book we will use the word 'creator' to refer both of them.

Rider-Waite Tarot deck consist of 78 cards out of which there are 22 major arcana and 4 suits of minor arcana consisting of 14 cards each. Minor arcana suits are

**Wands** (Fire element/Aries, Leo, Sagittarius/Action),

**Cups** (Water element/Cancer, Scorpio, Pisces/Emotions),

**Pentacles** (Earth element/Taurus, Virgo, Capricorn/anything tangible),

**Swords** (Air element/ Gemini, Libra, Aquarius/Communication).

To begin reading one must shuffle the cards, cut the deck three times and then select a card spread. There are many card spreads a reader can choose from such as CELTIC CROSS, 3 Card spread, single card (Yes/No) etc.

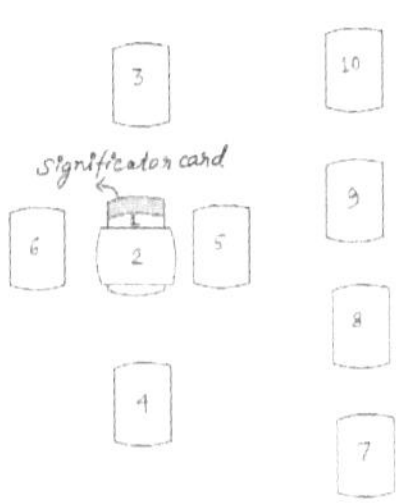


Celtic Cross Spread

Choice of the spread is as per tarot reader's discretion. Below is a three card spread(Past, Present, Future) for demonstration :

Think of a query/problem statement/ signification/person for which you want the guidance and lay the cards in the above fashion. Card 1 denotes the past situation for the query, Card 2 denotes the present situation, Card 3 will denote what is coming in near future/possible outcomes. Reader can pull out further cards from the deck for clarification in case he doesn't understand the themes or lack conviction for any of the three cards.

This book delves into the themes of 22 major arcana cards for better understanding.

# The Fool

| **Symbols** | **Possibilities/ Significance** |
| --- | --- |
| Fool | Mercury/risk taker/ foolish. |

| | |
|---|---|
| White rose | significance of innocence/ purity. |
| Standing on ledge | risk/foolishness/ unaware/leap of faith. |
| Dog | warning the person about the danger. |
| Bag | suggest journey/ short travel |
| Sun behind the person | going against the gain/ travelling to west /opposite to Sun. |
| Keywords | Mercury, Dog, Sun, third house of natural zodiac, innocence, naivety. |

| Themes prominent | Explorer, traveler, risk taker. |
| --- | --- |
| Zodiac sign | Gemini. |
| Nakshatra | Mrigasira. |
| Planet | Mercury. |
| Tarot meaning | new adventure, travel, risk taking, foolishness and themes of Mrigasira nakshatra. |

# The Magician

<u>**Symbols**</u>

<u>**Possibilities/ Significance**</u>

| | |
|---|---|
| ∞ | infinity symbol/ unbound / limitless. |
| Sword(on table) | air element. |
| Cups | water element. |
| Pentacles | earth element. |
| Wands | fire element. |
| White tulip | peace/ creativity. |
| Red rose | love/passion. |
| Magician | person who shows tricks with hands/ craft work. |
| Keywords | Handcraft, manifestation, creativity, magic, passion, limitless creativity. |

Card is a depiction of manifesting ideas into something practical.

| | |
|---|---|
| Themes prominent | Tvashtr is the deity connected to Chitra nakshatra which represents the limitless creativity of the nakshatra. |
| Zodiac sign | Virgo. |
| Nakshatra | Chitra. |
| Tarot meaning | manifestation, a trickster, creative person and themes of Chitra nakshatra. |

# The High Priestess

| **Symbols** | **Possibilities/ Significance** |
| --- | --- |
| Date palm | denotes fertility. |

| Pomegranate | denotes fertility because of many seeds/ beauty and eternal life/ association of bhumi devi(connection with mars). |
| Pearl/Crown/Full Moon | desire to be a mother/queen. |
| Pillar 'B' | Boaz |
| Pillar 'J' | Jachin |
| | (B&J are pillars of Solomon's temple). |
| Crucifix | connection with Jerusalem/ Christianity. |

| Script 'TORA' written upside down | sacred document in Judaism (meaning law of God 'TORAH'). |
| White and black colour of pillars | waxing and waning of the moon/ menstruating cycle of women. |
| Crescent moon at bottom | in Judaism and in many other beliefs it is a representation of someone who is not a mother yet (or virgin). |
| Veil with water likes waves | to put it in a euphemistic way the creator used white waves instead of colour red. |

Flower petals holding the chalice above the pillars image is similar to ovaries (refer to fig below).

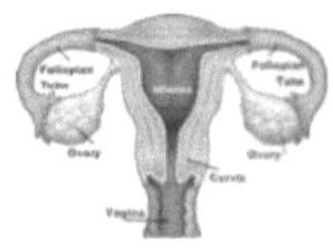 

Themes; Pillars Boaz and Jachin are the front two pillars of the first temple of Jerusalem built by King Solomon. In female anatomy the two pillars represent the fallopian tube. When a female becomes mother she becomes her higher self (Goddess). Final clue was to read the card in reverse order just how Hebrew read scripts (upside down). Once the card is reversed it represents the female reproductive organ. Overall theme suggests a female is trying to become a mother but not yet successful. Solomon temple might have a fertility clinic which was a secret.

Once Venus becomes mother ("Moon") she gets the respect of a queen as she provided heir to the throne and therefore elevates her respect. This belief was quite prominent during the era of kings and queens across many faith. Efficacy of fruits such as pomegranate as well as date palm in helping pregnancy/conception has not been substantiated yet but the creator gives a clue regarding the same.

| Zodiac sign | Aries. |
| --- | --- |
| Nakshatra | Bharani. |
| Tarot meaning | low fertility, pregnancy, secrecy, fertility clinic, secret knowledge and themes of Bharani nakshatra. |

# The Empress

## Symbols

Crown with twelve stars

## Possibilities/ Significance

queen's crown/ queen for all seasons.

| | |
|---|---|
| Scepter in right hand | royal figure/queen. |
| Cushion and pillows | comfort/leisure. |
| Female gender enclosed with a heart | feminine grace. |
| Clothes has image of pomegranate | fertility/youthful. |
| Crops at the bottom | barley/wheat etc. |
| Trees in the background as well as waterfall | abundance of nature. |

Themes; The card is a depiction of Ruth; wife of Boaz (the wealthy landowner of Bethlehem in Judea and relative of Elimeech). Elimeech was Naomi's late husband and father-in-law of Ruth. Ruth was the widow of Mahlon prior to marriage with Boaz. Even after death of her first husband Mahlon, she didn't abandon her mother-in-law. Ruth's devotion and loyalty impressed Boaz which resulted in their marriage.

| | |
|---|---|
| Zodiac sign | Libra. |
| Nakshatra | Swati. |
| Planet | Venus. |
| Tarot meaning | abundance, comfort, devotion, feminine qualities and themes of Swati nakshatra. |

# The Emperor

| Symbols | Possibilities/ Significance |
|---|---|
| Crown | king / head of institution. |
| White beard | old age/wisdom. |

| Orb/globe | symbol of power or domination. |
| Scepter in right hand | a scepter is always there with the king or royal lineage. |
| Ram head on four corners of the chair | mountain goat. |
| Sabatan shoes with left knee visible | shoes used by knights. |
| Dry mountains in background colour | fire element. |

Themes: the image talks about the first emperor Charles Magne or Charles the Great. He was a knight, later he became an emperor to rule the western Europe. The mountains and ram head stands for power and strength. Charles was born before marriage and also had a brother. When his father died, Charles and his brother co-ruled but after brother's death, he became the sole ruler.

| | |
|---|---|
| Zodiac sign | Aries. |
| Nakshatra | Krittika. |
| Tarot meaning | hotshot, authority figure, warrior and themes of Krittika nakshatra. |

# The Hierophant

| Symbols | Possibilities/ Significance |
|---|---|
| Three tier tiara | king/religious head/powerful figure. |

| Two fingers of right-hand pointing upwards | instructions/verbal judgement etc. |
| A papal cross | it represents the tree of life ; Kabbalah. |
| Red garment | symbol for status/power. |
| White sandals at the bottom of feet | connection with cult/religious institution. |
| Two semi bald people standing in front | suggest old people. |
| Two keys symbol below the sandals. | keeper of some secret item or knowledge. |
| White lilies on shirt of right person | purity/innocence. |

Red roses on shirt of left person — creativity/passion.

Mosiac engraved on both pillars — mosiac matches the arm of Pope Paul V (refer to fig below).

Themes; Card depicts Pope Paul V.

Although Paul V assumed office at a later stage (around 55 years) but he was vigorous and youthful for his age. He was obligated to none. He ensured that every right earned by his predecessors was not violated. Also criticized for nepotism. He enforced rules strictly and therefore a number of disputes. Two clerics were arrested by state Venice; Scipio Saraceni (Canon of Vicenza) and Brandolino Valmarino(abbot of Narvesa). Oligarchs of Venice wanted the trial to happen in non-religious court but pope Paul V wanted it in religious court. Two were accused of rape and homicide.

Paul V even thought of raising his own army but stopped due to Holland. After a certain time, king Henry IV of France settled the dispute between Pope Paul V and Venice.

Pope Paul V opposed the theories of Galileo who came to accept the Copernican model of the Universe. He made sure Galileo to be imprisoned for indefinite time as his research and theory goes against the clerical knowledge. He ordered new institutes for education and charity.

| | |
|---|---|
| Themes | Strong religious beliefs, opposition to research, education and art, youthful, very strict. |
| Zodiac sign | Cancer. |
| Planet | Jupiter. |
| Nakshatra | Pushya. |

| Tarot meaning | religious conviction, nepotism, influencers and themes of Pushya nakshatra. |

# The Lovers

| Symbols | Possibilities/ Significance |
| --- | --- |
| Sun in background | light/daytime/new day(beginning). |

| | |
|---|---|
| Different shades of hair of the angel like figure | fire and water/ cooler and warmer/ blessings and curse at the same time. |
| Wings | resembles archangel Raphael. |
| Twelve leaves on trees | twelve months of a year/twelve zodiac sign. |
| Fruits on the left tree | apple/orange/ mango etc. |
| Naked man and woman | innocent/naive/ child. |
| Snake on the left tree | serpent/Rahu/ corruption/ temptation. |

Mountain

separation between the man and the woman/ separation between the angel and man(woman) or both.

Themes; it resembles the story of Adam and Eve being evicted from the heaven (garden of Eden) to the mortal realm for falling victim to temptation. Both Adam and Eve were creation of God, Eve was made from Adam as a companion(more of a sister) but they ate the forbidden fruit and engaged in sexual intercourse which got Eve pregnant. Hence cursed by the God to live life as mortals. However, being the creation of God they were blessed as well. Open hands denote getting your desires into your own hand (loosely related to Hasta Nakshatra). It was the idea of Eve to explore the fruit once the serpent motivated her. Planet Venus gets debilitated in Virgo (6th house of natural zodiac). Pain, labor, difficulties are also denoted by 6th house of natural zodiac.

| | |
|---|---|
| Keywords | Incest, blessing, curse, difficulties, open hands, fulfilment of desires. |
| Zodiac sign | Virgo. |
| Nakshatra | Hasta. |

| Tarot meaning | temptation, passion, love and themes of Hasta nakshatra. |

# The Chariot

## Symbols

Castle on left and castle on right

## Possibilities/ Significance

castle on right looks like Babylonian castle.

| Canopy/palanquin with stars | someone royal or important person. |
| Crown with an eight-pointed star | king/head of army. |
| Two crescent moons on shoulder | cycles of moon/someone youthful. |
| Chariot wheel | chariot/transport. |
| Wings of victory | used in Roman legion. |
| Linchpin image in front of the chariot | linchpin used in chariots wheel. |
| White sphinx and black sphinx both tail inwards | white and black represents clear answer/no grey area. |
| King's wand or javelin | a weapon |

Theme; The card is a depiction of young Alexander's arrival in Babylonia. He was not a jew by race but still he had a lot of influence on the Jewish culture. The story goes by the name of "The Gordian Knot". A knot tied by Gordius; king of Phygria. As per the prophecy whoever unties the knot becomes the ruler of Asia. Alexander the Great used the linchpin of a yoke to loosen up the knot and then untied it therefore fulfilling the prophecy. The sphinx tails represents the knot that has been untied. Knot means 'Gandanta' in Vedic equivalent.

Keywords        king, gandanta, warrior, "The

| Zodiac sign | Leo. |
| --- | --- |
| Nakshatra | Magha. |
| Tarot meaning | easy solution to a puzzling problem, youthful figure, solution hidden in plain sight and themes of Magha nakshatra. |

# Strength

| Symbols | **Possibilities/Significance** |
|---------|-------------------------------|
| ∞ | infinity/unbound/limitless. |
| Background | sunny day/morning. |
| Lion as a pet | courage/valour/limitless courage. |

| Forest on mountains | probably the lion is petted out in the wild. |
| Female petting a lion | lion tamer. |

Themes; One needs to have headless courage to do this act. Male lion is animal representation of the nakshatra Purva Bhadrapada. Goddess Durga's mount is also a lion. Most of the lion(or tiger) tamers are Purva Bhadrapada prominent individuals.

| Keywords | Lion tamers, headless courage, mount of Goddess Durga. |

| Zodiac sign | Aquarius. |
| Nakshatra | Purva Bhadrapada. |
| Tarot meaning | Individual with extreme courage, situation demands your strength and themes of Purva Bhadrapada. |

# The Hermit

| Symbols | Possibilities/Significance |
|---|---|
| Lantern | light source/enlightenment. |

| Twilight/dark/night | darkness all around/ignorance of the soul. |
| White beard | old age/wisdom. |
| Cloak | for protection from cold weather/ conceal  identity. |
| Stick | support for walking/self-defence. |
| Snowy mountain | no man's land/ isolation. |
| One feet visible | may be left/right feet is either damaged or hidden. |
| Standing on the highest mountain peak | highest achievement/ looking at the bigger picture/bird's eye view. |

| Hermit | sage. |
| --- | --- |
| Themes | highest of enlightenment, occult, one footed person. |
| Keywords | Sage, isolation, enlightenment. |
| Zodiac sign | Pisces. |
| Nakshatra | Uttara Bhadrapada. |
| Tarot meaning | introspection, isolation, looking at the bigger picture and themes of Uttara Bhadrapada. |

# Wheel of Fortune

| **Symbols** | **Possibilities/ Significance** |
| --- | --- |
| Books | Ledger of karmic records/Akashic records/empty records(karma cleared or just started a new cycle). |

Clouds

Inner symbols

‘TORA’

hidden from the
material world/veil
which obscure what
happens behind.

Hebrew for
TORAH.

If these letters are

read separately then

confusion. Choosing

only four alphabets

'TORA' as the word

of God.

The four books above each represented by

a mythical creature are four foundations of

any religious/divine law. Vedic equivalent is

the Vedas (Rig veda Arthava veda, Yajur

veda, Sama veda).

Lines within the inner circle looks like

spokes of a cycle, it shows more

microscopic view of the outer circle. Vedic

equivalent to :-

Aranyakas; rituals, observances

Brahmanas; Commentaries on said ritual

Samhita; Benedictions, prayers, mantras

Upanishads; philosophical narratives and
dialogues

Four symbols Alchemy symbols namely
sulfur, Mercury, Water and Salt present in
the image.

|  | Overall theme suggest divine |
| Themes | laws, guidance as well as |
|  | karmic wheel. |

| | |
|---|---|
| Keywords | religious laws, guidance, karmic wheel, rags to riches (riches to rag). |
| Planet | Jupiter |
| Zodiac sign | Cancer. |
| Nakshatra | Punarvasu. |
| Tarot meaning | changes ahead, nothing is permanent, rag to riches (or riches to rags),  divine laws and themes of Punarvasu nakshatra. |

# Justice

| Symbols | Possibilities/ Significance |
| --- | --- |
| Sword | weapon. |
| Crown with a gem | king/royal/head/ authority figure. |

| Scales | properly balanced/ merchant/law/ justice. |
| Pillars | courtroom. |
| Right foot visible | |

Theme; the card is a depiction of the famous judgment of king Solomon. Balanced scale shows unbiased judgement and the sword is the clue. The story goes like this;

Once two mothers and one child came into Solomon's court of justice. Both mothers claimed the child as their own. To give justice king Solomon ordered to cut the child into two pieces and give each mother a piece. On hearing this, the real mother pleaded not to cut her child rather than to give it to the other woman.

As a result of this, king Solomon caught the deceptive woman because a real mother would never want her child harmed. Therefore justice was not only served but seen as well.

| | |
|---|---|
| Keywords | Justice, Judge, Courtroom, 9th house. |
| Zodiac sign | Sagittarius. |
| Nakshatra | Uttara Asadha. |

Tarot
meaning

justice, courtroom, judges
and themes of Uttara
Asadha.

## The Hanged man

Card depicts a man hanging upside down
by his own choice.

Sukhracharya despite being a better teacher
than Brihaspati was asked to teach the

Asuras(demons). To prove his worth Sukhracharya did a penance by hanging himself upside down to learn the mritsanjeevni vidya from lord Shiva. Indra observing this felt insecure about his position and sent his daughter Jayanti to disturb the penance of Sukhracharya. When Jayanti failed to disturb him, she lit a fire below Sukracharya's head in an attempt that the smoke will deter him but still it couldn't break his penance.

Similar myths is present in Norse mythology: -

Odin (one eyed all father God) hanged himself on the tree Yggdrasil for nine days by inflicting himself with his spear (a sacrifice of himself to him). He travelled the underworld and gathered all the wisdom in such a way that the realm of the dead refused him to stay and sent him back to the mortal realm.

| Keywords | sacrifice, occult knowledge, penance, undeterred. |
| --- | --- |
| Planet | Venus |
| Zodiac sign | Pisces(Venus exalted) |
| Nakshatra | Revati |

| Tarot meaning | Penance, undeterred motivation, sacrifice and themes of Revati nakshatra. |

# Death

## Symbols

Priest praying
before death

## Possibilities/ Significance

for mercy.

| King fallen on the ground | died/can't escape death. |
| Sun setting in the background | end of era/death/ destruction of lineage. |
| White rose on the flag | white rose is used for purification/ death/re-birth/ resembles the house of York(refer to fig below). |

White Rose of the
House of York

Themes; it represents the death of king Richard III (the last of English king) and the 'War of the Roses'. The extinction of the male lineage happened with the death of Edward Plantagenet, 17th Earl of Warwick. Edward's daughter Elizabeth of York became the first queen consort of England (Tudor dynasty).When Edward's youngest son was killed, the lineage of York ended and that of Tudor dynasty began.

| Keywords | Death, uprooting lineage, end of an era. |
| --- | --- |
| Zodiac sign | Sagittarius. |
| Nakshatra | Mula. |
| Tarot meaning | death, transformation, end and a new beginning, uprooting status quo and themes of Mula nakshatra. |

# Temperance

| Symbols | Possibilities/ Significance |
| --- | --- |
| Angels with wings | symbol of sol on head. |

| Letters on chest below the neck | Hebrew. |
| Triangle symbol inside the square | fire/passion. |
| Transferring liquid from one cup to another | water/some liquid that needs mixing. |
| Yellow iris flower at the right bottom | Fleur-de-lis(association with France)/Greek goddess of the rainbow. |
| One foot on land and another dipped in water | Achilles heel analogy. |
| Sun on hill side | |

Yellow iris is a poisonous plant but also has medicinal value (although not substantiated.

Theme; The angel is Goddess Iris twin 'Arke'. Iris takes nectar of immortality to other Gods from her chalice. She gets the water from the river Styx to serve the Gods. Iris has golden wings. Her twin sister Arke had Iridescent wings which was cut by Zeus before casting her into Tartarus after the battle between Titans and Olympians. Arke sided with the Titans whereas Iris sided with the Olympians.

Arke's wings were given as a gift to Peleus and Thetis on their wedding day.

Thetis later gave them to son Achilles.

| | |
|---|---|
| Keywords | God of nectar of immortality, healing qualities, knowledge of medicine, Achilles heel, subtle weakness. |
| Zodiac sign | Aquarius. |
| Nakshatra | Satabhishaj. |
| Tarot meaning | healing qualities, healer, Achilles heel and themes of Satabhishaj nakshatra. |

# The Devil

| Symbols | Possibilities/ Significance |
| --- | --- |
| Batwings | not human/ demon/lucifer. |
| Beard | old age. |

| Horns above head | goat horns/ description for Capricorn zodiac. |
| Letters on right hand palm | Hebrew, |
| Vulcan salute | live long and prosper. |
| Claws | of a bird/deformed figure. |
| Statue near left hand close to the fire | statue is prominent when looked upside down. |
| Fire at the tail of male figure | passion/sexuality. |
| Pomegranate at the tail of female figure | fertility/virginity. |
| Chains on neck tied to altar | a wilful prisoner as the chain is loose. |

The statue in the fire resembles the daughter of Jephthah playing string instrument (refer fig below).

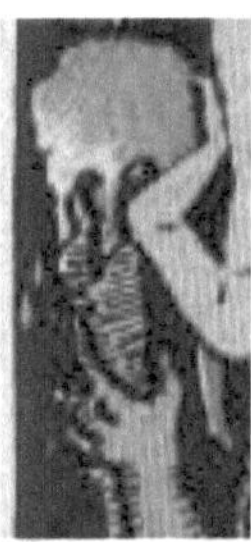 

Despite the vow to sacrifice his daughter in fire Jephthah allowed her to live with her lover but kept the fact hidden. The significance of loose chain tied to altar shows that Jephthah wanted the world to assume that the vow is kept. Jephthah's body was dismembered which are buried in numerous places. It is also depicted in the card that the legs are melting or shedding.

He was an outlaw king. He may be a criminal or a devil but not for the sacrifice of his daughter. It is because his daughter lived and may be people got to know only the half story of it. Jephthah had only one daughter therefore no continuation of lineage.

Themes; issues between father and child, loss of lineage, rogues, thieves, child of a prostitute (Jephthah) and no clue of father. Jephthah life revolve around themes similar to Ardra prominent personality. However, the card above depicts the consequence of a vow as well as breaking it.

| | |
|---|---|
| Keywords | Consequences of vow, hidden secrets, self-sacrifice, musical instrument. |
| Zodiac sign | Capricorn. |
| Nakshatra | Dhanistha. |
| Tarot meaning | vows, devastating consequences, misrepresentation, devil or labelled as a devil and themes of Dhanistha nakshatra. |

# The Tower

| Symbols | Possibilities/ Significance |
| --- | --- |
| Crown | king/status/ position/ego. |

| Thunderbolt | lightning/Indra's Vajra/reference to Ardra nakshatra. |
| Sudden event(people falling suddenly/in shock) | eight hose of natural zodiac. |

Theme; it is a depiction of Babylonian castle that crashed. Peoples' ego were huge and intelligence low which is why they wanted to reach the heaven by building a very high castle (the idea behind Babylonian castle). It is similar to Indra's fall from grace (high horse).

| | |
|---|---|
| Keywords | Tower, fall from high place, crushing of ego, sudden event. |
| Zodiac sign | Scorpio. |
| Nakshatra | Jyestha. |
| Tarot meaning | bolt from the blue, catastrophe, losing esteemed position and themes of Jyestha nakshatra. |

# The Star

| **Symbols** | **Possibilities/ Significance** |
| --- | --- |
| Seven cluster of stars in the sky | perfection/ completion in Judaism, seven is a spiritual number in different faiths as well. |

| Eight star is brightest | eighth avatar/ number eight in reincarnation/a newborn baby is circumcised on the eight day. |
| Stork on the tree | a bird in Judaism considered for child birth/ purity. |
| Pitcher | for carrying water. |
| Pouring water on the ground | nourishing/ bathing/wasting water. |
| Naked woman | bathing/cleaning. |

Letters formed by water poured from
pitcher of left hand of the
female and between her legs:

-

Geth; one of the five city of Philistine, there
are five ripples in the pond water.

Themes; The card is a depiction of king
David watching Bathsheba (wife of Uriah
the Hittite) naked while she was bathing.
David got her pregnant and also got her
husband killed. King David was the

youngest child (eighth child) of Jesse, he killed the Goliath of Philistine. David of Israel was a shepherd, a musician and later became a king. He had eight wives and many children.

| | |
|---|---|
| Keywords | secrecy, youngest child, attraction towards other mates, many wives and children, defeated a larger than size enemy, someone who rose the ranks from a very humble background. |
| Zodiac sign | Taurus. |

| Nakshatra | Rohini. |
| --- | --- |
| Tarot meaning | catching someone's eye, lust, larger than life personality, fatal attraction and themes of Rohini nakshatra. |

# The Moon

| Symbols | Possibilities/ Significance |
| --- | --- |
| Poles at both ends | representing north and south/cycles of moon. |

| Moon with sixteen primary rays and sixteen secondary rays plus displeasure on face | may be close to an eclipse. |
| Shedding of dews(fifteen dews) | fifteenth day of moon cycle. |
| Fox imitating a dog | deception/cunning. |
| Crayfish | a bait to differentiate between the fox and the dog. |

Themes; The card talks about deception. The fox eyes' is on the crayfish(food) and he is not howling therefore shedding his skin to reveal his true identity. It's a card that suggest to put a bait to catch the deception. Dog howling at the moon out of fear/warning of hidden danger.

| | |
|---|---|
| Keywords | deception, cunning, shedding of skin. |
| Zodiac sign | Cancer. |
| Nakshatra | Ashlesha. |
| Tarot meaning | deception, con-artist, bait and themes of Ashlesha nakshatra. |

# The Sun

| **Symbols** | **Possibilities/ Significance** |
|---|---|
| Sunflower blooming | sunflower always look at the direction of the Sun. |

| Sun is bright and strong | exalted position of Sun/Sun during noon. |
| A red flag as used by a jockey | flag of identity/ victory. |
| Naked kid riding a horse | a kid who has innate skills of riding or bonding with a horse. |
| Keywords | horse tamers, exalted Sun, child, jockey, Ashwa. |
| Zodiac sign | Aries. |
| Nakshatra | Ashwini. |

| Tarot meaning | youthful child, innate skills, victory and themes of Ashwini nakshatra. |
|---|---|

# Judgement

| Symbols | Possibilities/ Significance |
|---|---|
| Winged angel | Raphael/any angel/Hermes. |

Blowing a horn to alert/to communicate.

Ice mountain in background

Women, men, children up from their coffin and looking upward

Jewish flag

Calling towards heaven

Themes; it depicts the 'day of the lord', when the judgement begins few go to heaven and few go to hell. A rebirth/ closure of past/final outcome. It is similar to themes of taking souls to swargaloka in

Vedic equivalent. Pushan (deity of Revati nakshatra) is the ferryman that takes the soul to the swargaloka (heaven) over the river crossing yamaloka(hell). Greek equivalent for Pushan is Hermes.

| | |
|---|---|
| Keywords | messenger of Gods, Ferryman, day of the lord, verdict. |
| Zodiac sign | Pisces. |
| Nakshatra | Revati. |
| Tarot meaning | verdict, final outcome, rewards or punishment and themes of Revati nakshtara. |

# The World

<u>**Symbols**</u>

<u>**Possibilities/
Significance**</u>

| Four species lion,bull,human,eagle | four pillars of a foundation/ Purusartha(dharma, artha,kama,moksha) /foundations of astrological natal chart. |
| Naked female | Goddess. |
| Two wands; one in each hand | dance of the divine. |
| Knot in full circle | Ouroboros/serpent eating its own tail. |

Themes; The card depicts the beginning as well as the end. Every beginning has an end and every end has a beginning. It is the inevitable nature of the karmic cycle which is responsible for birth and death. Planet represented is Saturn.

| | |
|---|---|
| Keywords | World serpent, full circle, purna, sunya. |
| Planet | Saturn |
| Zodiac sign | Not applicable. |
| Nakshatra | Not applicable |
| Tarot meaning | re-birth, whole or void, repetition, orchestration of divine order. |

When not only our actions but even our words and thoughts are a response to an external stimulus then we are within the divine leela. Escape from Lord Vishnu's leela is inevitable even for the enlightened being but, they manage not to fall for others' leela.

# Glossary

| | |
|---|---|
| Nakshatra | lunar constellation |
| Bhumi devi | Goddess of earth in Hinduism |
| Gandanta | knot |
| Swargaloka | heaven equivalent in Hinduism |
| Yamaloka | hell equivalent in Hinduism |
| Rahu | north node of the Moon |
| Tvashtr | a deity, celestial architect in Hinduism |
| Brihaspati | teacher of Devas(Angel) |
| Shukracharya | teacher of Asuras(Demon) |

| Mritsanjeevni | knowledge of bringing the dead back to life |
| --- | --- |
| Achilles | a warrior in Greek mythology |
| Durga | a deity in Hinduism |
| Indra | a deity in Hinduism |
| Vajra | a weapon used by Indra |
| Ashwa | Sanskrit term for horse |
| Pushan | a deity in Hinduism |
| Purna | Sanskrit term for completeness |
| Sunya | Sanskrit term for emptiness or void |
| Purusartha | purpose of human being |
| Dharma | sustainable way of living |

| Artha | economic prosperity |
| --- | --- |
| Kama | desires |
| Moksha | liberation or emancipation |
| Vishnu | creation itself, consciousness, a deity in Hinduism |
| Shiva | a deity in Hinduism |
| Zeus | God of sky in Greek mythology |

# References

1.Brihat Parasara Hora Shastra, R Santhanam, ISBN-13: 9788188230600, Ranjan Publications, 2008

2.The Book of Nakshatras ; A Comprehensive Treatise on the 27 Constellations, Prash Trivedi, ISBN: 8170820588 (ISBN13: 9788170820581), Sagar publications, 2016

3. https://en.wikipedia.org/wiki/ Book_of_Ruth

4. https://en.wikipedia.org/wiki/
Charlemagne

5. https://biography.yourdictionary.com/
paul-v

6. https://en.wikipedia.org/wiki/
Gordian_Knot

7. https://en.wikipedia.org/wiki/
Judgement_of_Solomon

8. https://en.wikipedia.org/wiki/David

9. https://en.wikipedia.org/wiki/
Richard_III_of_England

10. https://www.encyclopedia.com/
people/philosophy-and-religion/biblical-
proper-names-biographies/jephthah